Windfalls

Susie Wild is author of the poetry collection *Better Houses*, the short-story collection *The Art of Contraception* listed for the Edge Hill Prize, and the novella *Arrivals*. Her work has recently featured in Carol Ann Duffy's pandemic project WRITE Where We Are NOW, *The Atlanta Review*, Ink Sweat & Tears and *Poetry Wales*. She placed second in the Welshpool Poetry Festival Competition 2020, was highly commended in the Prole Laureate Prize 2020, was shortlisted for an Ink Sweat & Tears Pick of the Month 2020 and longlisted in the Mslexia Women's Poetry Competition 2018. Born in London, she lives in Cardiff.

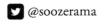 @soozerama

Blog: https://susiewild.blogspot.com/

Praise for *Better Houses*

'Susie Wild's *Better Houses* announces a new, highly distinctive and exciting poetic voice. [...] The author's balance between opening the door for the reader, and then hitting them with the poem's highly original approach to language and a slightly slant way of looking at the world, make these poems highly entertaining and rewarding. [...] an accomplished and auspicious debut...'
– Ink Sweat & Tears

'reels gorgeously from a restaurant to the seashore to the night sky [...] an unfinished journey through the experiences and signs that tell us we're home.'
– *Planet International*

'exuberant and smart [...] Half-remembered, half-invented, but wholly charismatic.' **– Wales Arts Review**

'Wild clearly has a sense of fun. Her poem, 'Pub Crawl Date' – cataloguing a nine-pint epic evening out – had me chuckling out loud. So too, 'The Bed Testers'. But, in my view, Wild is at her best when she is more serious and, to this end, there were several stand-out poems. [...] Similarly, there is a Plath-like forensic quality to 'The Lash Museum' which I also really enjoyed. It opens with "A gutsy Cornish wind / slammed the caravan door shut, / skinning a birthmark, / my head / a blood fountain." The poem's protagonist is then raced to hospital for attention and when the stitches are removed, she keeps them as morbid reminders of her pain: "clumped lashes a-flutter / in a plastic pot."' **– *New Welsh Review***

'As the title hints, Susie Wild's book *Better Houses* touches on some of the pressing concerns of the era (the housing crisis, social inequality). In 'Gentrifying the Area' she reflects on the rate of change ("three short months") that puts "tumbledown terraces" "on / the up, like the house prices". The poet reflects on her part in the process. She presents herself as the artist type whose cultivation of an area increases its value [...] Forced out in search of lower rent, the poem ends: "There are worse ways to be going, going / gone." It's an interesting angle to take and reflects the book's insistence to make the most of things, being whimsically enthused or tuttingly aggrieved with one's (always temporary) lot in life.' **– *Poetry Wales***

'Perhaps this is the message she wants to leave us with, the importance of opening doors and allowing for reintegration within an individual as well as across relationships through decency and kindness. Readers of all types will find something marvellous here.' – **Gwales**

'These poems are spells whose words bewitch the ordinary and transform the objects and routines of our human world with their word-magic.'
– **Gillian Clarke**

'The world shifts and transforms itself in these subtly disconcerting poems: words into bees, surgical stitches into mascaraed eyelashes, a fossil oyster into a lover's toenails. The effect can be darkly sinister or exuberantly witty, but it's always new and refreshing. This is an exciting and assured poetic debut.'
– **Matthew Francis**

'Susie Wild writes with poise and precision about the places we inhabit, casting a benevolent spell over her reader.' – **Samantha Wynne-Rhydderch**

'The voice is concentrated, urgent; the material is often tender, even domestic. There is no contradiction in this. The poems come from raw edges of the spaces between people, and a sense of how provisional the tender things can be.'
– **Philip Gross**

'Poems carefully built to be inhabited.' – **Cynan Jones**

Windfalls

Susie Wild

PARTHIAN

Parthian, Cardigan SA43 1ED www.parthianbooks.com
First published in 2021
© Susie Wild 2021
ISBN 978-1-912681-75-4
Editor: Zoë Brigley
Cover design by Emily Courdelle
Typeset by Elaine Sharples
Printed and bound by 4edge Limited, UK
Published with the financial support of the Welsh Books Council
British Library Cataloguing in Publication Data
A cataloguing record for this book is available from the British Library.

For those blown down,
May you rise again.

'I'm goin' on the mountain, gonna see my baby
But I ain't comin' back, well, I ain't comin' back'
– Merle Travis

CONTENTS

I:
THE CARNIVORE BOYFRIENDS

Now I exist in the realm of light again, I understand
there are times when it is necessary to approach

a blazing house and enter, times when I must open
my eyes wide and let in every quickening flame.

– John McCullough, from 'Sungazer'

The Liminal Hours

A chase of messages illuminates my screen
through the small hours. *Did I just see you?*
I'm sure I glimpsed you dancing, that green
dress, the way you tilt your head to admire

the view. These banshee hauntings
my poor abandoned dates, lost lovers?
What made them to conjure me?
The grade of rain? Do I slink? Do I down
a familiar side street in one port city or other.
                                          Leave

as they lean against a crowded bar, raise a glass
to their lips, too far, too drunk, to catch more
than a flick of my strange-coloured hair?
Do I lean into another under an umbrella

linger to clinch a kiss, taxi-vanish?
Where are the visitors who turned up
at my door with bunches of flowers.
Those who called me *Fire, Aubergine,*

Flower Girl? Those who held
my hand over a Sunday matinee film or
cheap wine carafes. I see a queue of them waiting
for a gig or a bus or me. Some mouth words

that mist in the rain before they reach my side.
Where are the ones who ghosted me, who swear
they glanced me in the liminal hours?
All those I've yet to spook?

The Carnivore Boyfriends

vary in their attitudes to prepping meat
and veg separately, disagree
on what constitutes a meal.
Boyfriend A cooks steaks
during vegan book group.
Boyfriend B mopes, anaemic, through morning
TV. *I did tell you*— I stop
myself, prepare all the meals
                for peace again.

Some are lapsed vegetarians,
a fad taken up for younger girlfriends
before Boyfriend C got bored of all
the chopping, pans and *fucking*
wasted time. He chooses takeaways,
restaurants, bars, where
the menu will not cater

for us both. They are all complaining.
I offer grapes
with cheese and crackers, butter
a couple of them up.

Boyfriend D and E still dabble, but rarely
cook. Boyfriend F stocks the fridge
with tofu, brings me apples,
wake-up coffee.

He'd rather kiss my flesh than fork
steak. I dig for cutlery hidden in socks.
I check his hands for knives.

The Vegetarian Helps Slice The Ham

Mum is wearing her white jacket, white hat,
green apron tied in a bow at her back.
I stand behind our shop's deli counter
beside her, aged 11, in a green tabard,
my mousy hair French-plaited, pulled out
of school three weeks before summer
break to help slice the ham. She cannot
lift it. She has broken her elbow, dislocated
a shoulder. I say *she has*, but she *fell*,
perhaps from a push by my brother, landed
badly. Insists she *slipped* in the stockroom.
So my job, instead of classes, is to lift
the joints from their display trays,
peel back the clingfilm of breaded yellow ham,
that blush-pink meat, of honey-roast glaze,
of pastrami – sliced thin – and set the machine,
switching places to let her operate it, legally
too young to cut flesh, break bodies.
Yet not much older than him.

In this battle, there won't be many hugs

It is the night I step out
    of Central Station to unboxed violence.
        The night the usual taxi rank, on shut down,
            forces me to cross to an unlicensed car.

The night my driver's door opens
    at the traffic-jam-junction, the stalled
        red lights. The click as the door in front unlocks. His sudden
            lunge forward, the fast words, a swung fist at man on the street
            on exiting the other car— caught cold, and I watch

                screen-separated inside the taxi
            until my driver reclaims his seat, slams
        his door. The lights flash amber, green and as he leaves
      my brain catches up with my eyes. I think 'Red.'

Say 'Stop.'
    'Pull over… I want you to pull over. NOW.'
        I begin my eight count: '1, 2, 3, 4…'
            He finally knocks out the engine at a patch
              of scrub by the prison. As I unbelt

              he heavyweights

              my belongings from the boot;
            punches my phone from my hand to blur
        attempted mugshots, is out of sight
     by the time I am upright, alone, seeking
number plate, car make, details. My next move.

The Special Officer

We catch looks like bullets across
a German metal band. A mutual friend,
that you know better, comes over to chat

me up. But you are the curve
ball that follows on my city meander.
A night off from working the festival

to enjoy bands takes us down to the sea
and back. You buy all the drinks, as we blag
you into this gig, then another.

Somehow, we're all back at someone's house
by 10pm, inevitable as the riptide
at Llansteffan. Your friend, still trying

to change my mind, runs me a bath and I leave you
both to your male chat for a while, splashing
about in blue. Later I tell you

someone told me it was safe to swim
in the estuary. I tell you about the current,
how strong it was, but I got out, survived.

You tell me about the wars you've served in.
Villages wiped out, 250 people, tied
to their partners, the men shot, the women left

alive thrown over a bridge into the river to drown.
You point to the shrapnel scar on your face,
reveal much more, hidden under the skin.

You tell me things you say you've never told
anyone else. How in your studio you battle
a different kind of metal. Welding gates and fire

escapes. For one night, you don't let me go.

The Disappointment

was all talk and no trousers,
sofa-sick and duvet-dick,

all those late-night romp
attempts at role play. Now

he's asking for
a sexy nurse's outfit.

Yet a bad back ails him, a wife
ails him, life ails him.

Now I'm out of reach,
I only have to tell him

I'm painting my toenails
in the bath to get him hard.

To leave him
w/ailing.

Brockley Cross

Remember when Christmas filled
our window from October to February,
its tinsel-bright, streetlight level gaze.

How the letting agent left his motor running
when he took us to our viewing – the getaway
driver. We woke to mice drowned
in our carpet of night-before glasses, and I

no longer flinched finding roaches in my underwear
drawer. We slept on plastic and air
inside our festival dome tent to escape,
leaned the rotten bed frame on the landing

instead. When we showered,
water rained into the dry-cleaner's downstairs,
and he would bang the ceiling, complain
when our band rehearsed in the daytime.

Do you remember how the landlord never fixed
anything? How, at night, the orange walls turned black
with the scuttle of Kafka; how I had to skip

college classes, scrub until my fingers bled.
We were young and happy, with our Poundshop
Christmas Day, our chippy dates, candles and cans, our flat-
roof 'garden' to look out at a London version of sky,
the light pollution hiding the stars.

The Optimistic Nihilist

introduces himself as that at the speakeasy bar,
and agrees to keep me company. He reminds me

of jet, from his hair to his snake sheen;
the jut of his jaw, the neck tattoo, it sends me giddy.

Later at the sofa where the others snort
speed, I turn it down, my life

running fast enough. We kiss, leave quick,
taxi to his side of town.

He is shady, renegade
as he takes out a gun, pretends

to shoot me, then tucks it safely away again.
The problem is idiots, he says, then switches his focus

to me, the danger disappears to doe-eyes,
as he wraps us up in blanket, skin to skin.

The Knotweed Remover

I can sort out your problem for you,
this stranger in a bar hands me a business card, winks.

I wonder how he knows: though I've not seen
the knotweed return, I hear it creak in the night. How can I

unroot it? Soon I learn his unknotting by day is replaced
with ropes after dark. *Sometimes you have to tighten first*

to loosen up. You can't always leave as cleanly
as you'd like. Though I wake to nail marks, had to dig out

in the gloaming, where it haunts, threatens regrowth. Invasive,
it taunts me: spray, injection, herbicides, stem. *It won't*

leave quickly. He surveys the damage: cracked tarmac, blocked
drains, undermined foundations: tries to calculate my decline

in value. 20%? 30? Knots scourge everywhere but nobody
is tying them: gut, shoulder, all the unlabelled boxes

under the stairs. *It can take three years so you'll have*
to be patient. And rich: £1500 for just a small patch

of weed. Experts suggest even that is futile. No cure.
In the house, in bones, the creaking grows

louder. Shoots appear wrapped in a strangle
of ropes, their small voices repeating:

untie me, untie me, untie me.

I like your face

he said, but please excuse mine
I have been burning the candle
at both ends, and now it is a melt
of wax, but you can place your thumb
prints here and here, claim me
as your own, if you'd like. Mostly
I'm not malleable, but fully formed,
yet there's room, at the soft edge
of things. There's room, for you.

He didn't bring me flowers

but fruit and exotic vegetables
leaving a pineapple on my pillow,

or standing, proffering an aubergine
from the doorstop, the exact shade

of my changing hair, or matching
the gloss of my new tights.

He'd give me pet names to fit
the gift of the hour. Pleased with his finds

bergamot, durian, custard
apple, kumquats, dragonfruit.

How they sounded and tasted
on my tongue.

Then he came spilling sunflowers,
a bouquet of seeded promises to break.

I haven't liked them as much since.

This Is Why We Can't

In trying to become / a perfectionist / I forgot how to be / myself, how to dress / like me, talk like me, object like me, / how to laugh. The man had / expensive taste / and spent too much on the things / we didn't need, / so if something slipped / washing the dishes or rolled off / the counter he would shout / *This is why we can't have nice things.* Stomp / into a room full of nice things. More / than I'd ever had before / as I shrank back / into the kitchen / into the suds of cleaning up. / Became less / and less / and less and less. / Nothing.

Traumatic Language

Come to   find   time has unstitched   whenever open   mouth
all can say   'Sorry'   a whisper   *Sorry sorry sorry sorry sorry sorry sorry*
Do not know why   sorry   what sorry for   Am a sorry   state   Yes
Bedraggled   inside clothes   Yes   unbrushed, curling into knots   Yes
Sorry sorry sorry sorry sorry sorry sorry   Repeat it like mantra   That look
it evokes Pity?   Contempt?   Worse?   *Sorry sorry sorry sorry*
sorry sorry sorry   Apologising for existing   feels that way   perhaps felt
for long while   *Sorry sorry sorry sorry sorry sorry*   like forgotten how to
speak like something   or someone   knotted tongue   Try to reach   out for more
       words   Wave clutched-hand   Scrabble tiles   still   only eight-
point score   out tumbles   *Sorry sorry sorry sorry sorry sorry sorry / Sorry sorry*
sorry sorry sorry sorry sorry / Sorry —

     sorry— sorry — sorry —

          sorry —

    sorry — sorry / Sorry

         sorry sorry sorry sorry sorry

                sorry //

When I asked my mother if she remembered

my bike, she said *No.*
No to the white frame with the clover emblem,
to the basket. No to Clover—?

No to the bike that was my world,
that I peddled fast to get away
from sibling shouting and scrapping,
far along the tree-dappled lanes
around our creekside village.

No to my blue bike, one high enough
to accommodate my long legs, gangle-
grown tall before my class caught up.
On this bike I meandered for miles, from home
to harbour, quayside to pontoon.

And no to the boy: louche, blond, tanned
and scuffed – *other* in some way
that I recognised – and that catching
caused us both to halt
our solo rides, one foot each
on the ground, as we talked.

Only I remember a familiar stranger
who told a teenage me
that I was free, nodding at my wheels, saying:
'Now you can go anywhere.' He flashed me
a cowboy smile, rode off, kicking the dust
to catch in the sunlight behind him.

Newly Single,

perhaps they would call it naive, to stand
at the bar alone talking to a stranger. Yes, he
was cute – you had no plan to go home with him,
but he was walking your way and it seemed safer

than walking alone. They might call you naive, when
his friend started after you both shouting, not to call
a taxi after all, but you were skint, which is how
you ended up here in the first place. Wasn't

your phone nearly out of credit? They'd say
you should have seen it coming: the escalation,
anger, frenemy revealed in the rush to the first
man's upstairs flat. No communal space but

instead a door opening to a corridor of beds,
an advance unwanted. And how glad you were
for your survival strength, the hand that reached
out shoving him, how you slammed the door

against his chest. They'd tell you to be glad
of the police CCTV that tracked you when
the second man pursued grabbing your wrist,
leaving nail marks, blood, bruising that you

didn't notice until the police car picked you up,
drove you home to safety. Perhaps you should
have pressed charges. Spoken to someone.
But you didn't.

Grindr

Swipe right? I am more of a left-
side-of-the-bed girl. Waking up
with jaw ache from too much action
in my mouth
all through the night before.

These are the hours where I don't
remember my dreams. These are
the hours where, when I sleep,
I grind myself down. Bruxism.
A slow defiling of a smile.

I grind myself down.
I grind myself down.

Amber

Is that dropped
gaze caught in
nightclub shadows

a lover's green light?
His dawn farewell:
guitar-rough hands,

still the softest touch
of a smoke-signal
in our shared ashtray.

Burton's Boy

The spawn of Tim Burton, you are
all Edward Scissorhands bird's-nest
hair and couldn't-care-less.

Matchstick frame. Shambolic flair.
You're a fucked fairytale.
You're not really there

but disco-dancing,
a swaying sparkle in scarves,
a preening prowling dandy-lion.

Ale drinker, big thinker,
you *Vogue* in drainpipes,
slide down them at dawn.

The Topless Bassist

is an exotic species that leaves me
perplexed. I want him: I tell
him this too much.

He is slow to forgive
my prima donna. We are
mistimed or misnomers.

Our work shifts are incompatible
but we are not. An invitation arrives
to a free gig he is playing in my city.

The band hug me, though he does not.
He drinks my red wine on stage
to impress me. But at 9pm we leave,

him for work, me
for the place that is home.
Just for now.

Please Do Not Blame Me For This

I am tired of it now, despite the held hands
over tables. The turning up with gifts
of wine and wreaths, a real tree.

This is a poem I am not allowed to write
but here I am. Writing it.

How to approach me

1. Do not rush or creep
2. Articulate your movements
3. Say: *I am behind you*, but know this is no pantomime
4. Do not rush or creep
5. Articulate your movements
6. Say: *I am going to hug you now, is this okay?*
7. Do not rush or creep
8. Articulate your movements
9. Keep your voice gentle and low
10. Nobody needs to jump

Eye Contact

He ducks my gaze this time,
as we walk back to our shared
neighbourhood. He says
he is all out of eye contact, for now.

Given he has met my widened eyes
for almost 90% of the evening,
this seems fair.

He says sometimes he can't read expressions.
I tell him I'll help him
to read my face.

On our third date in a week,
we both become less awkward
with each other, asking first-date questions.

We hold hands, walk forwards,
eyes on the destination.

Something Like Blue

In the welcome petrichor, I think
of him. How his pigment-less eyes scatter

light, reflect blue, the same as sea, sky, my sunflower eyes
mixing pigment and scattered light, the colour varies

day by day. On the beach at Swansea Bay he told me
my butterfly ring suited me: it seemed

ready to take flight. Though the man
on Koh Chang refused

to tattoo me, said butterflies
did not suit me, I should not

flit here,   flit there,

            but settle,

be still—

Look at the blue morpho Grandpa Tom netted,
now framed on the desk. Look for the blues

of my father's eyes, fading

generations of us

all just   trying

            to catch

blue.

II:
WINDFALLS

Windfall

1: something (such as a tree or fruit) blown down by the wind
2: an unexpected, unearned, or sudden gain or advantage
— Merriam-Webster.com

'Windfalls are named for the instrument of their falling. You know, it isn't much of a leap from (of) fall to fail and an even littler leap from fall to jump. I used to look at the railway tracks every day.'
— Jenn Ashworth, *Notes Made While Falling*

Nude, smoking, in the dawn doorway

he stands, or
leans against
the door frame, light spills
around him, haloing
as he moons me. *The husband,*
inhales smoke,
exhales smoke,
takes deep breaths
surveys his terraced territory:
newly cut trees,
soil awaiting seeding.

Nude reclined,
I watch these in-between hours,
neither bed nor
morning. We reject time,
make our own
routines. Days and nights
punctuated by this: the flare
of a lighter, the nude
smoking, in the kitchen
doorway. The taking
of deep breaths:

surveying.

Windfalls

Next door's apples now overhang
the garden fence above the sunspot
where I sit and read in the afternoon.

The boughs heavy with fruit flushed
by the heatwave, dropping like flies as I watch,
ignoring the piles of bills before me.

Though tomato plants shoot
taller and taller, blossoming
yellow, new flowers
still wilt in the corner.

I imagine sitting at the table later,
being rained on; each apple
a small bomb.

The patchy grass, the path, the veg beds
are drowning in windfalls
alive with insect feeding and decay.

The Handkerchief Tree

I stumble upon it walking, physically distanced
from groups of two-by-two air-seekers.
Some are masked, gloved-hand in gloved-hand,
on government-sanctioned daily outings. I desire-line
off the main path, boot-stomping
the green between river and public.

This lone dogwood's branches are fresh-
blooming, large white bracts waving a truce.
In Cardiff's Camellia Garden they hang
small heads like sacrificed virgins.
Or doves, breeze-disturbed, uncertain
of finding peace.

Most will not see them.
These faux flowers won't last
the frost. Others call it *The Ghost Tree*,
laundry strung outside
in gothic dreams, a warning
of something sinister underfoot.

I bear yet cannot bear
witness to it. I circle thoughts,
pacing around and around
the trunk wondering
which name applies to it today
in rare May bloom?

In the arrest of this brief flutter,
what message does it have?
What slogan to take away:
peace, Othellian misunderstanding
or surrender? These dove-posted letters
ask me to take notice.

I've been wanting to write to you about the trampolines

but somehow I keep getting distracted
by thoughts of the flood, the way the trees in Bute Park

were like bathers waving or drowning,
bare arms in high winds,

how the walking dogs were confused
at the new pond extensions – their now-swamped paths.

I've been wanting to write to ask if you'd seen them
airborne, bouncing as far as we'd once dreamt we could.

Remember? When we practised and practised, sometimes
for so long and so high and laughing so much we wet ourselves

just a little, but never said. All that mattered then was the height,
the leap away from land, from everything, and so,

when I saw the wrecked ground as the waters
ebbed, though I felt the devastation of those flooded homes,

of everything lost, my first thought was how I wished I could
reach you to tell you about these flyaway trampolines,

stopping trains in their tracks, causing the chaos we'd wanted.
Stopping the world, so that we could show off

our balance, our sailing grace,
our flight.

Mademoiselle Albertina

i.m. Louisa Maud Evans, 1896

There she is in the balloon, her self-sewn sailor's suit,
straw hat. All fourteen-and-a-half years of her, rising
for the parachute descent on Cardiff outskirts, her rapturous
return to the Exhibition crowds, this horse-and-carriage heroine.

Watch as the Balloon Girl careers over Newport Road, speeding,
as the wind drops and lifts her to a greater height. See how,
at 5000 feet, adrift over the Bristol Channel, she unclips
the hope that the parachute will save her.

How it spreads like silken wings, carries her from land, hits
water. How thirty soaked pounds of cloth and wood weighs
her teenage frame, drags her deeper, deeper, drowned.
The body washes up near Nash three days later.

A failed leap of faith. This aeronaut is grounded
in Cathays, her lichened tombstone paid for
by the public who watched her rising, rising,
and watched her fall.

Everyone Got Married

He was a cupped hand
to the cigarettes she'd quit

but taken up again, only to burn
the time they spent like candles.

She cast lines and nets,
caught wishes,

the glint of beaked mackerel,
the silver lining to a flesh-pecked bone.

Beyond their boat, stars were strung
across the late sky:

bauble-eyed, they tried
to drop anchor.

The Peaky Fucking Blinders

'... is there some gene that codes for the old Travellers' huge hands, or is it the
fact that they've grafted and shovelled and built and been injured and scarred
and punched their way into massiveness?' – Damian La Bas, *The Stopping Places*

I charmed you like a horse whisperer but,
instead of Appleby, I met The Family

in a Cardiff park with cherry blossom confetti
in my tamed curls, a paper bouquet in my hands,

the sparkin' had already happened
and the Black Patch brothers,

in their dark suits, escorted me with broad
shoulders and shovel hands, our

shared mischief-spirit showing we were
from the same *atchin tans*. From

bride's side to groom's the Brum
accent flowed like fizz, friends

and family. And we were *cushti*—
The Peaky Fucking Blinders.

How Much Sickness Are We Talking, Exactly?

For Ben

For we've already had more than our fair share,
fevered and sweaty in our whirlwind love,
and are you sick of me yet, darling? As I fall
over, fall further into this, as a date
is set, as our goose is cooked, love?

And where is this health they talk of, this absence
of aching pains, these that I feel for the taking
of you, for the lack of you, here, by my side?
I would marry you daily, if I had enough dresses.
Whether you work in Aldi or add

the word Doctor at the start of your name,
even if I'm driving barefoot across America, trying
to learn your songs. Whether we've babies on the rug
and little else but this, love. And after all, these
setbacks are simply more stories we can tell.

Escape on Severn

In the shepherd's hut
we are top-tailed,
bed reading, wrapped
in woodburn
and tea cosy.

Outside nothing
but water – rain, river –
sheep and birds,
half-naked,
shivering trees.

For one whole day
we forget the city,
forget other people
exist, we hush

our hearts and selves,
play tiny house, where
the only waste
is composted.

The Starfish

'The sick ones tend just to fall apart in front of your eyes. An arm will actually break off and crawl away' – Jeff Marliave, Vancouver Aquarium biologist

I wake, arms spread across an empty bed,
hundreds of tiny feet reach for him, reach
to recall which of us is away from home,
lost in unfamiliar blankets. Those nights

when he is not there, when I wake cold
in Valencia at 8am, despite the rising heat
outside, five floors above the traffic, in blackout
night. Or in Wales, I wake
at 3, at 4, at 5, to no snoring,

no talk radio and cross the bedroom
to turn the heating dial up to low. He's on
shifts, cold-snap-busy at the wet shelter, breaking
up knife fights, nursing Spiced Zombie ODs,

brewing tea, 12-hour frazzled, spiny-skinned. We
starfish, regenerate our own limbs, every day
a reminder, we're not the worst off, are far from
the worst off in our mildewed house, the stained carpets.

Slowly we fix the broken things.

Transmission

5 January 2020

As the news and your father broadcast wildfire
in Oz, from Oz, we pack up red and gold
tinsel and baubles in Wales, take down the tree,
unaware of how much worse is yet to come.

The Key Worker's Wife

'Good Morning!' He greets my lounge arrival
        a little or a lot after his nightshift return.
'Good Evening!' I reply, rubbing my eyes.
        I leave the curtains shut to the street, open

those facing the garden. He cracks
        a can of beer, turns on the talk
radio that lullabies him to sleep,
        or outrages him to crack another can.

We sit together in this half light,
        recount our hours apart, mine uneventful
by comparison: Netflix vs. knife fight, bubble bath
        vs. raving sheela na gig, silence vs. sirens.

Soon it is his time to lie down,
        snatch a few hours before the next
shift while I draw the rest of the curtains,
        wake to a reassuring soundtrack of snores.

I am cutting the lawn with secateurs

I have a bin-bag full of clothes etc.
ready for when charity starts up again.

I have a pile of ironing I am still ignoring.
I have no need for straight lines.

I have tidied my underwear drawer.
I am judging the rest of you now.

I am cutting the lawn with secateurs
just to make the joy of the task last longer.

I have decluttered the bathroom
of old make-up and aged bottles.

The neighbours have begun learning
ukulele AND Spanish, badly.

I am cutting the lawn with secateurs.
just to make the joy of the task last longer.

Her Next Door

We used to think it was a game –
the knocking – something between
her and the young daughter:
a secret language or a kind
of Morse code. But

the knocking grew
louder and louder, not
just a knock to be let in,
not a special knock to say
'It is okay, darling, it is only me.'

But a frantic knocking, to our left,
an ever-more frequent knocking,
TAP-taptaptaptap-taptaptaptap-tap-tap
that seemed to grow with the bad
news on the radio.

TAP-taptaptaptap-taptaptaptap-tap-tap
on the front door, on the pipes
in the bathroom, on internal doors,
on the walls, our side, asking
her to stop. Until that time I saw

Her Next Door, child in hand, outside
locking and re-locking her door,
knocking the same knock:
TAP-taptaptaptap-taptaptaptap-tap-tap
before turning and walking away.

Him Next Door

Armed with secateurs I cut
the blackened heart,
the black-fly crusted centre,
from the runner bean tepee
and this too flowers.

Butterflies return as
gladioli and marigolds wilt
to their fainting couch, blue
cornflowers and red dahlias
taking over the display.

Half the garden breathes
and blooms in the heatwave,
the other half rots: the difference
of given space and light, stoked
at staked support.

As I feed what remains
Him Next Door comes out
peering through a gap
in trellis and foliage to nod
at the sunflowers.

They turn their big heads
in his direction, towering
over the fence like security lights.
I took a photo, he says, captioned it:
The neighbours are watching.

The Long Night Moon

It is not quite full / the Child Moon / last waxing / gibbous moon of Winter / but low and bright, cold / and catchable in the clear sky / walking to Co-op at / the bidding of a husband / quarantined in the attic marked / unclean until further notice / she was free / to buy provisions to toss / at him, walk the busy, far-too- / busy parks choosing / off-peak times / washing *out damn* / *spot* from hands and surfaces / until his negative test result / 10 days of house arrest / *just in case* / 2020's last gift.

The Cancelled Honeymoon

We dream of azure so I paint
our rented garden's rotting shed doors and table
Summer Sky blue and make Greek salad.
We sit alfresco and, though it isn't the same,
there *is* a heatwave: it *is* closer

than we hoped. Each day I tweet
our #FakeHoneymoon #Corfu: swimming,
mountain hiking, olive groves, boat trips,
the high-speed hydrofoil to Albania,
the waiter whose eye I caught – smashed

plates – while instead we sofa-sit, listen
to the news. Refund-pending, as rain
buckets, the husband researches fresh
destinations: Cuba, Greece, I lose track

of my furloughed days. Our plans for May
involved more cocktails, more nudity, not
this endless scrolling, this disappointment
as we clink Retsina, Tripadvise better times.

Curfew in Chania

At midnight we follow the bracelet / curve of the Venetian port back / to our room, our balcony above / the waterfront, best seats / in the house, as below us / the promenade restaurants / and bars clean up, stacking / tables and wheeling bins, as / police parade, flashing / their lights but sounding no / sirens, as all calms to stillness. Even / the water traffic stalls, no tourist boats / and no fishermen at this hour, just / the moon and the lighthouse and / the sweeping of brooms, the closing / of blinds, and us, clinking glasses, / over it all.

The Swallows and the Swimming

At dusk I have the pool
to myself – the panoramic view,
until the swallow show joins me
for a parabolic dive-dip. Beating me
to a pre-dinner drink.

In chlorinated light-rippling blue
they zip, loop and swoop
from edge to edge as I breast-
stroke to the horizon of hills
and back. Such freedom, such glee.

The Red Moon

I wake to blood in my mouth and spit out hazy panic. Two slug-like clots cupped dark in my hand. *Unexpected side effects include blood loss*, the small print had said. *If symptoms continue after 48 hours, please seek medical attention.* This is the first time. At the sink I discard, rinse fingers and gums and move to the balcony for air. I tiptoe though my husband is not easily disturbed from sleep. I pour a glass of Retsina from the half-empty bottle abandoned earlier and watch the sturgeon moon set, red melting into the sea, down the hill from our hotel. The town otherwise in darkness, quiet. This – the first time I've seen the moon set. This burst of loud colour burning in the stillness.

She does not scream at hauntings

It is raining in the bedroom again,
bucketing over the fourposter
and the ghosts are boohooing about
damp nightdresses and pointing fingers:
she does not scream at hauntings.

The window flings itself open
and they bow and curtsy unthanks,
turning heads to dagger glare
before huffing off, searching dry
lodgings, more thrilling frights.

In the corner she cowers,
unnerved by the weather, the quiet
inside, the loud beyond.
She curls and awaits the inevitable
knocking. *Here it comes—hush now—*

Here it comes—

How to Be a Recluse

I set up Zoom meetings with the dead
seeking invites into their spotlit rooms
their tidy, book-lined corners.

I tried to get Greta Garbo on the phone,
but she declined to comment. Said
she wanted to be alone.

I DM'd Harper Lee to ask how to be
more of a private person, the message
remains unread.

I tried to catch up with J.D. Salinger,
to see if he still practised a vegan diet,
ate in the kitchens of diners, if he ate out,
drove a jeep with the windows draped?

I clinked virtual baby lemonades
with Syd Barrett who told me:
all crazy diamonds like us need
is in the post. I waited.
I tried to shine on.

I nitpicked the parts-I-liked wisdom
of the *Hikikomori,* their single
room occupancy, their late-night feasts.

I gave up watching Westerns,
envying the cowboys their loner life
on the open range too much.

I tried to commune with the spirits
of hermits, cave and island-dwellers,
mythical creatures.

I sought enlightenment
but I was forgetting how to speak,
the silence settling around me:

I boarded up the windows,
unplugged the phone.

Death Comes Quickly

in my Robert Street garden, spreading
across the gaps left
by slow pruning
and uprooting plants
that did not survive
our honeymoon weather.

Back home and quarantined
I eke out my tasks:
one day I feed the last
morose sunflower,
on another I shout at the bugs
attacking the pumpkins.

The holly berries blush
in full display already,
courgettes finally have space
but are too late, waving
their little penis crops about,
the ivy everywhere unfurling.

It is 4:30 in the afternoon again, dear

and here we are, tangled up amongst the sheets
in your *Twin-Peaks*-red room, or is it my sycamore
green? We are heatwave-sticky, your cat an echo
of... ignore me, actually, dear.

You say it is always 4:30 somewhere, but
in these hours of drawn-against-time drapes
and waning-moon picnics, things
are all upside down, dear.

At Cardiff Beach they've employed speedboats
to choppy the sea, shipped in sand and palm trees;
and though the sun melts behind buildings, don't
be fooled. It will rise again, dear.

I prefer it

when you are more yourself

We should go

after the initial shock

to the hospital. It's been a long time

and you are always so brave

to bleed – I know you say it is okay

beautiful?

I know you say it is still okay, natural in fact

but I…

but I worry, now, about how much

I want

I want to draw a line

to mark you safe from all we have placed

in our way.

How quickly we forget how to live

I am dressed as a handmaiden
in Tory-blue Britain,

my baker-boy capped head
not upturned, not held out,

but a gaze cast downwards,
disposable mask feeble

against a plague
of rain.

I cross emptied streets,
those few minutes from essentials,

to a front door more familiar
viewed from inside.

I am signing the wrong name again

or the right one spilling out
of boxed lines on the form.
My new name: too big to contain
here, or in my mouth.

Some days I forget who I am
supposed to be, flitting between
old and new personae, the bank
official name I use for one

job, the one I use for another.
I find a way to stop needing
new forms, sign my four initials
instead: unchanged, fitting.

Mr & Mrs Smith

They held hands as they climbed the mountain
of the night before: committing, booking a room, signing
the Visitors' book 'Mr & Mrs Smith', engaged
in enjoying one another. On the way down

the slope they spotted her ex first, scuttling up
the thorn-clogged path towards them, the cut-
through to their pub with rooms, the peak rising
behind it. A limp girl shrank into his shadow. Familiar

as a puddle. 'Well Hello There!' he bellowed, expectantly.
Mrs Smith looked down. 'Hey,' she replied. Then silence.
The ex's nod, surprised but curt. Both parties continued
to move further away from each other, ground conquered,

when she turned and caught him stalled
watching her aghast. Mrs Smith thought not
of deers and roadkill but of tectonic plates, of shifts
in gravity, of finally stepping away.

Heavyweight

We sat through rounds of silence,
in the lamplit side room, where the locals
thought me timid, him gregarious.
The wino at our other Sunday haunt declared
the same, and somewhere in my head cogs clicked,
That's not right, that isn't who I am, how it is.
I challenged him, silently.

After, in a limbo world of boxes in an empty house
too far out of town, the freight train rushing by the end
of the garden, I went to that pub for the warmth, on my way
back from town or Aldi, examining the boxing photos
on the walls, thinking of the ring upstairs, all those unspoken
fights we should have let blaze earlier.
A jab-hook-slip of words.

I came out of my shell, sheltering
from an emptied life, and the locals filled it
with tall tales and a turn on the jukebox, bought pints,
checked I was having a hot meal. Made space
for me at their table when I'd finished reading poems
in the lamplit room. Hedged their bets on the horses
and the misjudged dates I paraded their way.

So You Wanna Be a Boxer?

Fight and fight some more
Until you know the world is ready to receive you

In my school production
of *Bugsy Malone* I played
a Down and Out, not
Leroy the champion.

Now, thanks to the Government
Skills Test, I am outside
retraining as a professional
boxer in my rented garden.

Preparing, this Gypsy Queen
will rise like the Gypsy King.
Can you see me in my gym kit
and pigtails, feet moving

with dancer's muscle memory
to ballet second position,
a demi-plié into a steady two
o'clock, the back heel lifting
from the ground?

Imagine this patio a ring.
See me swivel, barre-less,
on my hips, bandage cloth
around poet hands, don
the red gloves. Ready.

I have to mean business
in my new role. I learn to jab,
to left hook, to right uppercut,
my cross fists thumping

the training pads. I learn
my best angles, the power
of the turn, the clean points
of contact for the win.

I learn to hide my face,
to block, to slip, to duck
the washing line. Skills
useful in this new age.

Watch me do my *Rocky* montage:
– there I am skipping rope,
– here running up snowy steps
outside City Hall,

– there wiping sweat
from my brow. At the end
of my session someone,
watching, says:

Eyes of a killer, watch her!

My trainer looks at me,

sees an opponent,

nods.

The Bell

Like pressing the buttons at museums, I like to call
Time at the bar, ladies and gentlemen please, to strike
the ding-ding-ding on the bell. To make them drink up after
a fair drinking-up time, to get them to scarper to more

trouble or home. I have stood between overgrown men
before, broken up fights, threatened to call their mothers,
their numbers Blu-Tacked behind the bar, thrown my young
size 8 self in their path, the men on shift all standing

back but watching. They know these boys don't
fight girls. I quote the number from memory
of the biggest lad's Mum. *Shall I call her, Jack?
Or will you go quietly?* He pauses, slow motion,

looks at me, registering the danger, downs his pint,
says *Come on lads, we should let her get her beauty
sleep or Smiler here will only refuse to serve us at all
tomorrow, let's go*. He puts his hands palms up

in a sign of truce. Or peace. Or both.

Wild Flowers

Now when we come together,
we splinter bones.

Our mirrored injuries
bloom across our feet,

as we find weight too hard to bear.
Outside September rays

have willed one surviving
sunflower tall, a spike of petals unfurls.

Two magpies chatter amongst the apples
still clinging to the tree.

The lawn, I've given up on,
burgeons pink with wild

strawberries, yellow with dandelion
like ripped knickers strewn

beneath the unseasonable laundry
strung out to dry.

Inside he watches the boxing
to distract from his pain,

waiting for petals
to break through the skin.

When They Dropped the Pollen Bomb

'The combined effect of warming temperatures and more CO_2 means that the amount of pollen in the air has been increasing and will continue to increase as climate change worsens.' – nationalgeographic.com

How we wept— drowning
British pavements
in a sniffle of tissues.

How we ached— cradling
heads and inhalers
to ward off further enemy attacks.

How we bled— our nose-plagued
millions in worst-case scenario
summer disaster.

How we cough-cursed— the rain
aiding infection, feeding the grass,
on false-flag days.

How we scratched— at throats,
begged for drugs, remedies,
felt very anti histamine.

How we sweltered— eyelids
like puffballs on red alert.

How we itched— for reprieve.

All That Burns

'Have you noticed I can't be around you in enclosed spaces?'
he says, driving me to work. 'But cars are fine?'
I ask, raising an eyebrow he catches in the rear-view mirror.
'Yes, cars are fine.' I notice he's shaking again. I Mona Lisa smile,
look out of the window at the coastal path of factories, the waste
incinerator, the polluted smoke from all that burns inside.

All I Have

They are still there –
the windfalls, rotting
in garden waste bags.
Still awaiting being taken
to the tip, months after
the asking.

The grass is getting taller,
the few neighbourhood cats
who'd been invisible here
until recently, now fight
over mice, voles, rats
– I don't want to know.

And two magpies, two urban
crows visit us like
an ark. Some days
it doesn't rain, and I stand
and take in all I have –
despite everything.

Car Wheels on a Gravel Road

After Lucinda Williams

We are in the car – Gibson on the backseat,
cwtched with our stage hats and dusty bags –
as we take a ride through the mizzle, along
the A470. Waterfalls and jawdrop views fly by,
familiar – still favourites, we *know* this road
and I lean back, my cowboy-boot-shod feet up
on the dashboard. The city crying dirt behind us.
Loretta's singing on the stereo. Waylon
Jennings and John Prine. We gallop
towards mountains, a first pint, the next gig.
Got folks in Llani we're gonna meet.

It is

your text's screen glow
'I'll be there in 10';

the glass emptying
while I wait;

the door creak, the freeze-
blast of January;

the dust catching
at the back of my throat;

the pub staffie, leaping
up for affection;

the lemons, curling,
by the till behind the bar;

the clean-smell
of your just-showered arrival;

the hand, shaking,
that lets yours hold on.

The Lit Match

Oh, she's naked again,
look at her stalk the stage
like a lit match, blazing.

Oh, she's conjuring better
houses then burning them down,
until the audience stands on ash.

Oh, she's turning up again
with her broken wings and wheels,
her demands. Perhaps she needs

a sherry? Some rouge for those
roots. It can be hard to hide your
true ones. Oh, my dear,

meet me outside the library
with a red rose. I'll be
wearing one too.

Born the Running Kind

With apologies to Merle Haggard

We were born ready to leave:
you packed your pockets like
I packed my bags and mind.

I'd pick the furthest places
I could think of: San Francisco
instead of uni, then Edinburgh

when I was convinced not to run
quite so far. Now, when you are fuming
I jump

on your lap, hold your shaking hands,
remind you that we don't always need
to run. Sometimes we turn, we face

it head on, and don't get mowed
down. We learn to stay still.

Afterword

This book is written for the women (or perhaps the people) who do not fit the happinesses that are planned for them. For the ones who find love late, the ones who choose not to or cannot have children, the ones who cannot see the appeal of being chained to the kitchen sink, the ones who divorce, the ones betrayed, the ones who find love on Grindr or Tinder and the ones who do not, the ones for whom dating is exhilarating and dangerous, the ones who are still looking for whatever it is they really need.

Notes

The Peaky Fucking Blinders – The epigraph is taken from *The Stopping Places: a Journey through Gypsy Britain* by Damian Le Bas (Vintage, 2018). The English Romani words *atchin tans* and *cushti* translate as stopping places and good or lovely.

Death Comes Quickly – More commonly known as herb Robert, this plant has been used in the folk medicine of several countries, including as a treatment to improve functioning of the liver and gallbladder and to aid healing wounds.

So You Wanna Be a Boxer? – The epigraph is a quote from the 1976 *Bugsy Malone* song of the same title.

When They Dropped the Pollen Bomb – The epigraph was taken from a 2016 nationalgeographic.com article written by Becky Little – 'Climate Change Is Making Your Allergies Even Worse'.

Acknowledgements

The Merle Travis lyric quoted at the front is from his 1951 song 'Nine Pound Hammer'.

John McCullough's 'Sungazer' poem features in his latest collection *Reckless Paper Birds* (Penned in the Margins, 2019) and I thank him for permission to use it here and for writing that book.

An earlier version of 'The Carnivore Boyfriends' appeared in *Poetry Wales* in 2020.

'In this battle, there won't be many hugs' placed second in the Welshpool Poetry Festival Competition 2020.

An earlier version of 'Brockley Cross' was published as part of Ink Sweat & Tears' 12 Days of Christmas feature 2020. 'Nude, smoking, in the dawn doorway' was shortlisted for Ink Sweat & Tears Pick of the Month in 2020. 'How Much Sickness Are We Talking, Exactly?' was shortlisted for Pick of the Month in 2019.

An earlier version of 'The Knotweed Remover' was longlisted in the Mslexia Women's Poetry Competition 2018.

'Burton's Boy' was first published in *Nu: fiction & stuff* (Parthian, 2009)

Thanks to Jenn Ashworth for giving permission to quote from her excellent book *Notes Made While Falling* (Goldsmiths Press, 2019).

'The Key Worker's Wife' and 'The Cancelled Honeymoon' were published as part of the WRITE Where We Are NOW project with Manchester University in 2020.

'It is 4:30 in the afternoon again, dear' was published by The Cardiff Review in 2021.

'Wild Flowers' was highly commended in the Prole Laureate Prize 2020.

'Car Wheels on a Gravel Road' is a great song and album of the same name by

Lucinda Williams. 'Running Kind' is also a great song, this time by Merle Haggard.

'It Is' was written at a poetry workshop with Rhian Edwards as part of Cardiff Poetry Festival in 2020, and after her poem of the same name in her second collection *The Estate Agent's Daughter* (Seren, 2020).

I thank you and you and you...

Thanks to my dear editor Zoë Brigley for her generous friendship and support in poetry and in life.

Thanks to Rich and Gill at Parthian for continuing to encourage me to write.

Thanks to the lovely publications and prizes who have picked my poems from this collection along the way and to all of the superstar hosts of events where I have been invited to perform. And those who have put me up too. You know who you are!

Thanks to all my wonderful groups of writers who have helped to shape some of the poems here in our strange plague year jumble of catch ups and in the years before: Heidi Beck, Mark Blayney, Emily Blewitt, Zillah Bowes, Emily Cotterill, Rhian Edwards, Julie Griffiths, Kali Hughes, Mab Jones, Rebecca Parfitt, clare e.potter, Marcelle Newbold, Kate North, Amanda Rackstraw, Tracey Rhys, Katherine Stansfield, Christina Thatcher and Hilary Watson. Thanks also to constant readers including Laura Bishop Reynolds, Stephen Clarke and Roberto Pastore.

Thanks to Louise Walsh for the boxing lesson and for her advice on the other boxing poems.

Finally, thanks and love to my favourites – there whether stealing my bed or 'trapped' in paradise, Swonzee, lockdown or non-stop nightshifts – Not-my-cat, Helen, Jon and Ben.